With best wishes
Walter J Weber

Signs of your Life

SPECIAL
T-BONE
60¢
WITH MEAT
$5.50

Humor and Fun in Signs across America

Walter J. Weber

Printed in the U.S.A.

ISBN 0-937959-89-8

Library of Congress Catalogue Card No. 89-90347

Published by Walter J. Weber, 36 West Roberts Road, Indianapolis, IN 46217, (317) 786-7251.

Publishing consultant:
Falcon Press Publishing Co., Inc.,
Helena, Montana

Dedicated to my darling daughter Susan Johnson, who succumbed July 4, 1988

Laughter promotes healing. Psychologists have learned that laughter reduces pain by releasing a type of hormone known as endomorphine. This is nature's own morphine.

Contents

Preface 6
Shoplifters 9
Warnings 11
Trespassing 20
Cities and Towns 23
Fishing 28
Parking 31
Speed and Auto 35
Food and Taverns 42
Love and Marriage 51
Dr. and DDS 53
Funeral Homes 56
Cemeteries 58
Restrooms and Sanitation 60
Money 68
Antiques 70
Advertising 73
Misinterpretables 74
About the author 96

Preface

After God created the world he made man and woman. Then to keep the whole thing from falling apart he invented humor. The good news is there is no ban on humor, laughter, smiles, and happiness. The best face lift in the world is free. It is a smile. Humor brings smiles. A smile is nature's best antidote for trouble. It brings rest to the weary, creates happiness, fosters good will, and is a sign of friendship.

Here is what Professor Herb True, University of Notre Dame, world-renowned educator, says about humor: "It takes humor power to make life complete. Humor has an instantaneous effect. It makes a person feel good. A relaxed attitude of friendly humor establishes a person as a welcome companion. Good humor and laughter are contagious."

Here is a comment about humor from Dr. Joel Goodman, editor of *Laughing Matters*, founder of the American Humor Association, and director of the Humor Institute: "Laughing matters! It really does! More than 200,000 people have attended our humor program on the positive power of humor. It is clear that people realize humor is a universal language. There are many reasons why we should be serious about humor. (1) Just for the health of it—laughter may in fact be the best medicine. (2) Laughter is the shortest distance between two people (according to Victor Borge). (3) Humor can maximize our problem-solving abilities. (4) Humor is a way of moving from—'grim and bear it' to 'grin and share it.' In other words, humor is a way of reframing reality, of moving from stress to opportunities to laugh.

"This is exactly what Walter Weber is doing with this book. By looking at reality—and finding humor in it—he invites us individually and collectively to lighten our loads. Walter's comic vision is wonderful—and his book indicates clearly that humor is a SIGN of the times."

Grateful appreciation is extended to the many individuals who have told me where to find certain signs or for sending pictures to me. Credit should be given to the many individuals who conceived the ideas and took time to prepare the signs so others could forget about some of their worries.

It is always a pleasure to learn about new thoughts. We must remember we become mentally dead when we stop learning. It will be a pleasure to learn about and to receive pictures of signs.

Walter J. Weber

Shoplifters

1

SHOPLIFTERS
WILL BE BEAT UP
OR PERSECUTED
WHICHEVER COMES FIRST

2

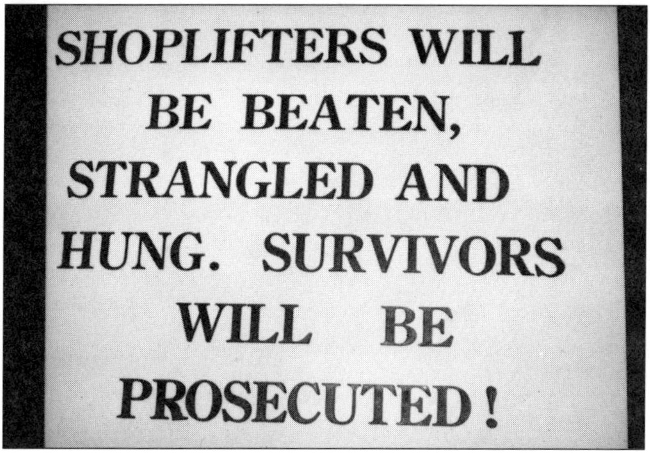
SHOPLIFTERS WILL
BE BEATEN,
STRANGLED AND
HUNG. SURVIVORS
WILL BE
PROSECUTED !

1
"I don't want to start any arguments. I just want to explain why you are wrong." "Running into debt isn't so bad. It's running into creditors that hurts."

2
"This man said he was scared. He got a letter from a guy who said he would break his legs if he didn't stop seeing the man's wife. 'Well, that's easy, all you have to do is stop seeing his wife.' 'Easy for you to say.' 'You like her very much?' 'That's not the point, he didn't sign his name.' "

1

ATTENTION
SHOPLIFTERS
WE WILL DEAL WITH YOU
HERE ON PREMISES
WE WILL NOT CALL POLICE
WE WILL CALL AMBULANCE

2

SHOPLIFTERS
will be cheerfully
beaten to a pulp

3

SHOPLIFTERS
WILL BE GIVEN A
FAIR TRIAL
THEN
HUNG

1
"Money isn't everything, but it sure comes in handy when you lose your credit card." "It's frightening to visit our IRS office. It shares space with a blood bank."

2
"I admire a good loser—as long as it isn't me." "Insure a busy tomorrow, procrastinate today."

3
"Our town is so small that the hospital has only one life support system—and that is coin operated." "Grocery bags are stronger now. They used to burst with $10.00 worth of groceries. Now they easily hold $40.00 worth."

4

BEWARE OF BULL
DO NOT ENTER THIS FIELD
UNLESS YOU CAN CROSS IT
IN 9.9 SECONDS. THIS BULL
CROSSES IT IN 10 SECONDS!

5

BEWARE
OF "OWNER"
DON'T WORRY
ABOUT DOG.

4

"Keeping up with the Joneses is not as bad as passing them on a hill." "My boss is mean, but he is fair. He is mean to everybody." "My boss gave me a day off for my silver anniversary, then said he hoped I wouldn't bother him for a day off every twenty-five years."

5

"Do you know why the fastest dogs live in Siberia? Because the trees are so far apart." "As people grow older, they acquire many things: leisure time, pleasant memories, and a sudden and intense interest in Polydent."

1

BEWARE
PLEASE REMOVE DENTURES, RINGS, & OTHER METAL OBJECTS, PRIOR TO ENTERING THIS PROPERTY WITHOUT INVITATION. THESE OBJECTS INTERFERE WITH OUR DOBERMAN'S DIGESTION

2

DOG IS OK
BUT
BEWARE OF WIFE

1
"Beware of the dog. He makes snap judgments."
"The noblest of all animals is the dog, and the noblest of all dogs is the hot dog. It feeds the hand that bites it."

2
"Dogs are dumb animals, but look who works so hard to feed them."
"The trouble with lots of speeches: the speaker gets paid when it should be the audience."

3

CAUTION
IRRITABLE
FARMWIFE

4

LEASED PARKING DAY & NITE
WARNING
DON'T SAY YOU DIDN'T SEE THIS SIGN
YOUR CAR WILL BE TOWED AWAY
IF YOU PARK HERE!
CONTACT POLICE

3

"The food editor received a call about how long it would take to cook a fifteen-pound ham. The food editor reached for the reference and said, 'Just a minute.' The caller said, 'Thank you,' and hung up." "A thoughtful wife is one who has the pork chops ready when her husband comes home from a fishing trip." "You are getting old when you don't care where your wife goes, just so you don't have to go along." "If at first you don't succeed, try doing what your wife said."

4

"Watch out for children, especially if they are driving cars." "Our boss is a real motivator. He motivates us to get to work on time by providing fifty parking places for seventy-five employees."

1

NO
HORSES
ON
SIDEWALK

1
"If you are beginning to encounter some hard bumps, be glad. At least you are out of the rut."
"I don't believe in fur coats. The only one who really needs a mink coat is the mink."

2

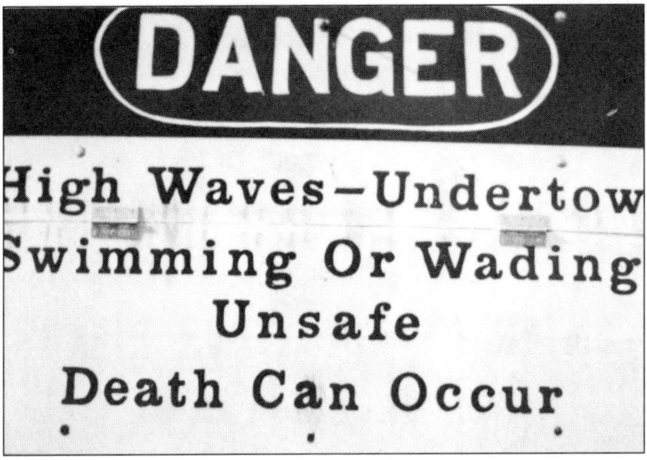
DANGER
High Waves–Undertow
Swimming Or Wading
Unsafe
Death Can Occur

3

WARNING
STAY OUT OF MY FIOWERS
AND FORGET THE DOG.
ITS THE OWNER YOU
BETTER BEWARE OF.

2
"Did you ever hear of safe death?" "Snow and adolescence are the only problems that disappear if you ignore them long enough."

3
"An added joy of giving instead of receiving is that you don't have to write thank-you notes."
"The only person with his problems behind him is a school bus driver."

1

KAPUAIWA GROVE
DANGER
FALLING COCONUTS
ENTER AT YOUR OWN RISK!
DEPT. OF HAWAIIAN HOME LANDS

2

ANY PERSON FOUND
ON THESE GROUNDS AFTER
SIX AT NIGHT WILL BE
FOUND ON THE GROUND
IN THE MORNING!

1
"I'm so behind that I am just now putting off the things I should have put off six months ago."
"Retirement is when you bend over to pick something up and wonder who lowered the floor."

2
"They said to work harder, you will be rewarded, and I was—with more work."
"I don't object to members of Congress receiving honorariums. It's the dishonorariums that bother me."

3

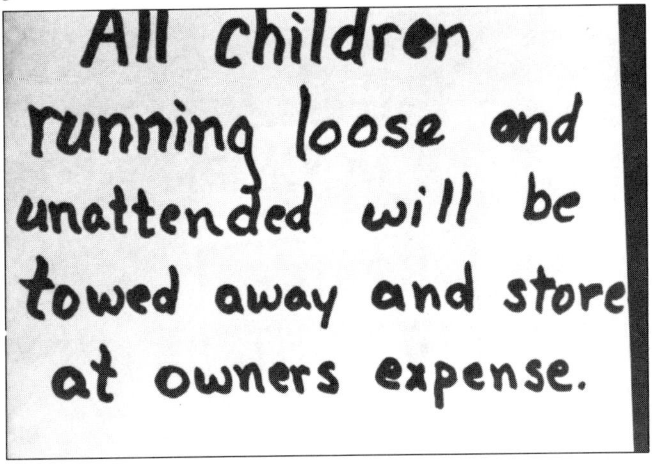
All children
running loose and
unattended will be
towed away and store
at owners expense.

4

ANYONE CAUGHT STEALING
TODAY WILL BECOME SAUSAGE
OR HAMBURGER TOMORROW!
DEPENDING ON FAT CONTENT

3
"An optimist is someone who tells you to cheer up when things are going his way." "There is no child so bad that he can't be used as a tax deduction." "Plan for next year. Send your dog to camp and your children to training school." "One should hide all valuables in the bathroom. With these teenagers, no one could ever get in there."

4
"Most people go on a diet with the wrong equipment—a knife and fork." "It's time to diet when your chin moves and the second one seconds the motion."

1

WARNING
BRIDGE
WEIGHT
LIMIT
ONE
TRUCK

1
How much does one truck weigh? In Custer National Forest. "Talk about progress. It took Columbus seventy days to go from Europe to the Caribbean. Today it only takes people seven hours to make the same trip. It's your baggage that takes seventy days."

2

BEWARE OF NUTS
CROSSING AHEAD

3

THIS PROPERTY PATROLLED
BY WATCHMAN WITH GUN
ONE NIGHT PER WEEK
YOU GUESS WHICH NIGHT

2

"The trouble with people who talk too much is they often say something they haven't thought of yet."

"As a prudent and careful driver, I'm sorry they raised the speed limit to 65. Let's face it—cars going 65 are much harder to pass."

3

"If you tell a man there are 300 million stars, he will believe you. But if you tell him a bench has just been painted, he has to touch it to be sure."

Trespassing

1

NO TRESPASSING
IN CEMETERY
VIOLATORS WILL
BE HAUNTED

2

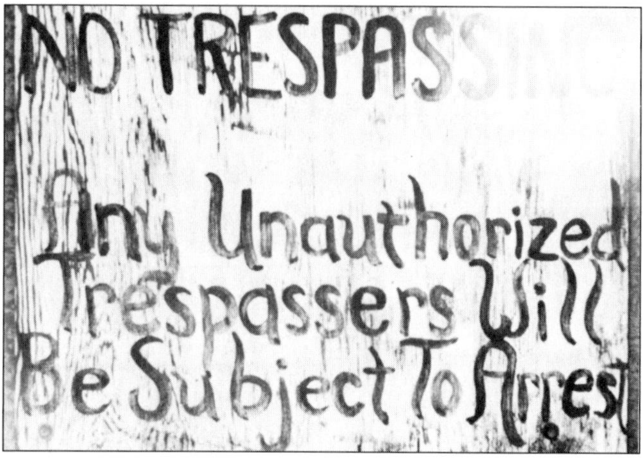
NO TRESPAS
Any Unauthorized
Trespassers Will
Be Subject To Arrest

1
A logical place for haunting. "I have reached the age when the best birthdays of all are those that haven't arrived yet."

2
Just what is an unauthorized trespasser? "Those who know the least know it the loudest."

3

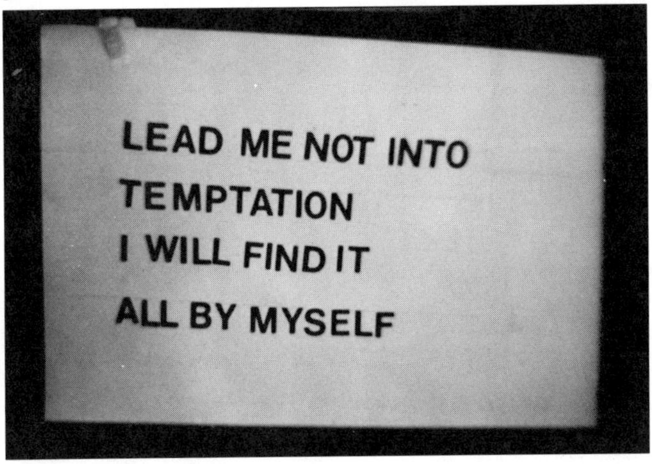
LEAD ME NOT INTO
TEMPTATION
I WILL FIND IT
ALL BY MYSELF

4

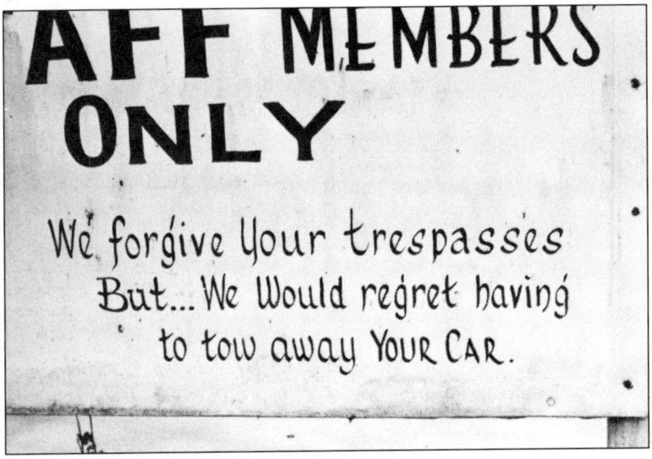
AFF MEMBERS
ONLY
We forgive Your trespasses
But... We Would regret having
to tow away YOUR CAR.

3
"I can resist anything except temptation." "You know you are getting old when your problem isn't resisting temptation, but finding it."

4
"The way of the transgressor may be hard, but it sure isn't lonely." "I'm not against capital punishment. There are a lot of people in the capital who should be punished."

1

TRESPASSERS WELCOME
HUNTING FISHING HIKING
TRESPASS FEE $200.00 PER DAY
PAY AT HOUSE 1 MILE NORTH

2

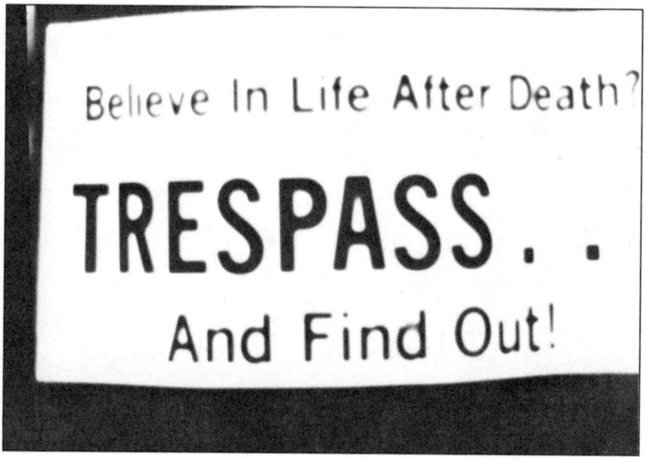
Believe In Life After Death?
TRESPASS . .
And Find Out!

1
"I am in the 50% tax bracket. I make half of the money I need to survive."
"Think small. Big ideas upset people."

2
"America is where anyone can become president. To become a supreme court justice is not so easy."
"Complaining about the weather? Suppose the government was running it instead of just predicting it."

3

PINCH - QUICK
ROAD
47

4

MILFORD
HOME OF 700
FRIENDLY PEOPLE &
3 OR 4 OLD GROUCHES

5

CATEECHEE 1
SIX MILE 5
S.C.
137
S.C.
93

3
Pinch and Quick are two towns in West Virginia. "I have lousy health insurance. They won't even cover heart operations. They claim it is elective surgery because you elect not to die."

4
"America is the only place where you can go on the air and kid the politicians, and where politicians can go on the air and kid the people."

5
Five miles to Six Miles. "The perfect journey is circular: the joy of departure and the joy of return."

1

HEADED THIS WAY
IT'S 24,934
MILES TO
WALL DRUG
TURN BA

2

ANCHORAGE
185 Miles
DRIVE
HOPEFULLY

1
Wall Drug claims to be the world's largest drug store. It started back in the thirties when the owner advertised free ice water near the Badlands.

2
Drive hopefully, but also carefully. "You are getting old when you are sitting in a rocking chair and can't get it started."

3

DRIVE CAREFULLY
BUFFALO IS
A One Hearse Town

4

WELCOME TO
BIGGAR
NEW YORK IS BIG
BUT THIS IS BIGGAR

5

GOLDVILLE
POP. 999 972
LESS THAN
A MILLION

3
You have heard about one-horse towns. This one is different. Buffalo, Wyoming, has a nice campground. "Most children today grow up very quickly. One day you look at your phone bill and you realize they are teenagers."

4
"A lot of people are buying Japanese cars, but not me. I will stick to a Ford, Chevy, Chrysler, or Olds. I don't believe in driving anything I can't pronounce."

5
The answer is the same with old math or new math. "The first crisis this couple had when they were first married had to do with the usual one night a week out with the boys. He insisted that she give it up."

1

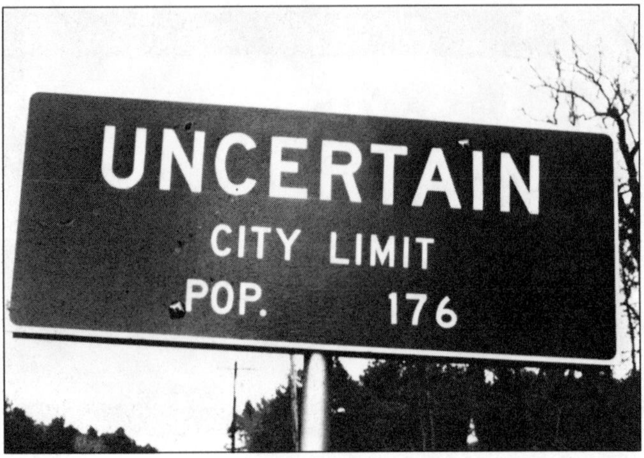
UNCERTAIN
CITY LIMIT
POP. 176

2

TOURIST INFO.
CADDO LAKE. UNCERTAIN TEX.
PHONE 214 789-3366

1

"Any politician will tell you that you can fool all the people some of the time and some of the people all the time, and usually that's enough."

2

You can get Uncertain information in Uncertain. They also have an Uncertain volunteer fire department in Uncertain, Texas.

3

WELCOME
MISSION
CITY JAIL
HEARTBREAK
HOTEL

4

NOTHING AZ.
POP. 4

5

WHEN YOU'VE SEEN NOTHING
YOU'VE SEEN EVERYTHING
NOTHING, ARIZ. HWY 93
INDIANA • 80
99C1740

3
The Mission, South Dakota, city jail serves as the heartbreak hotel—and it's free. "A successful man is one who makes more than his wife can spend. A successful woman is one who finds such a man."

4
Nothing, Arizona, is halfway between Phoenix and Las Vegas. "Some people with nothing to do still make a mess of it."

5
After you have seen Nothing, Arizona, you should go to Nowhere, Arizona, about 75 miles north of Phoenix. "You can't have everything. Where would you put it?"

Fishing

1

Welcome
TO
ENNIS
POP._473 PEOPLE
10,000,473 RAINBOW TROUT

1

"It's easy to spot a well-informed man today. He is totally confused." "The politician's speech would have been perfect if at the end he would have added, 'But seriously folks.' " "My life insurance company just inserted a reincarnation clause. They will pay if I die, but if I come back, I have to bring the money with me."

2

LICENSES
SUCKERS

3

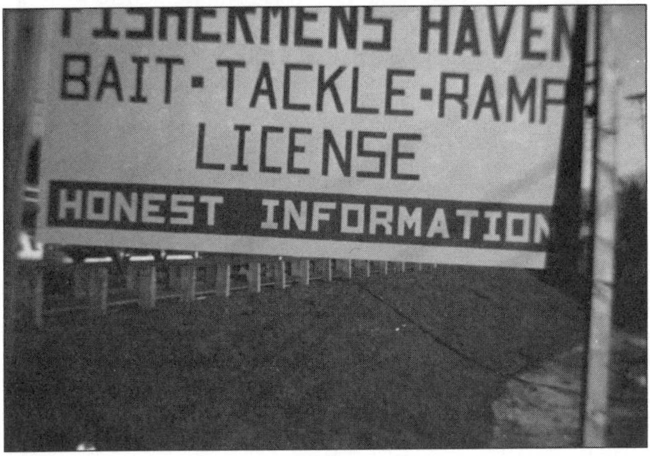
BAIT · TACKLE · RAMP
LICENSE
HONEST INFORMATION

4

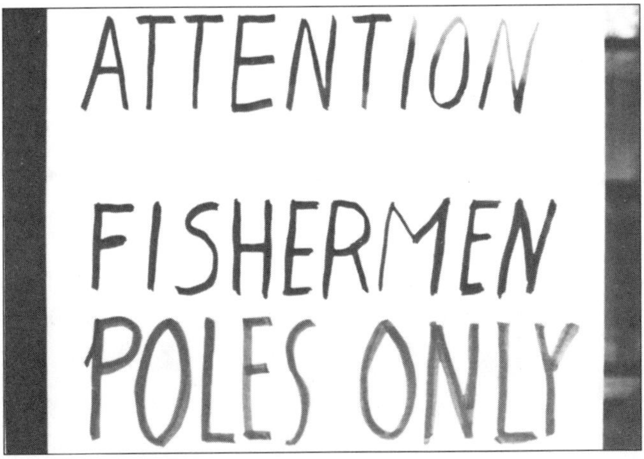
ATTENTION
FISHERMEN
POLES ONLY

2
Who buys licenses in Sioux Narrows, Ontario?

3
"Some people look for things to worry about. I met a man who wondered if the Declaration of Independence was notarized."

4
What about non-Polish people?

1

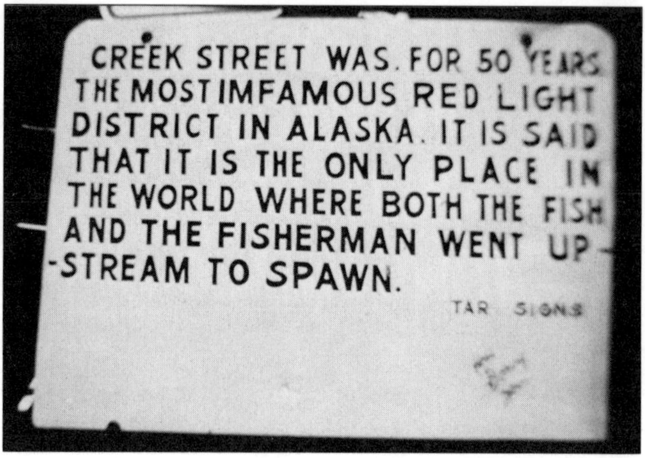
CREEK STREET WAS. FOR 50 YEARS
THE MOST IMFAMOUS RED LIGHT
DISTRICT IN ALASKA. IT IS SAID
THAT IT IS THE ONLY PLACE IN
THE WORLD WHERE BOTH THE FISH
AND THE FISHERMAN WENT UP-
-STREAM TO SPAWN.
TAR SIGNS

2

COLDBEER
FISH BAIT
VISA

1
A little humor in Ketchikan, Alaska. "I have an aunt who was married so late in life that Medicare picked up 80% of the honeymoon."

2
Does cold beer really make good fish bait? "What good is it to be the breadwinner, the guy who brings home the bacon, when my family wants to eat out all the time?"

3

UNAUTHORIZED
VEHICLES
WILL BE
IMMOBILIZED

4

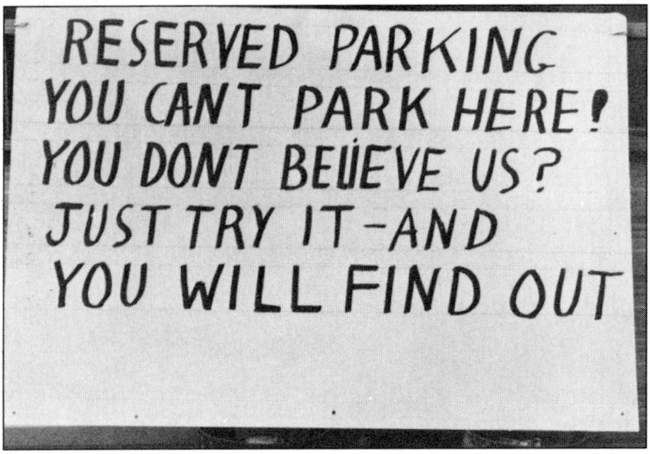
RESERVED PARKING
YOU CANT PARK HERE!
YOU DONT BELIEVE US?
JUST TRY IT-AND
YOU WILL FIND OUT

3
Be careful where you park in Central City, Colorado. "My airline has just accepted me into its 100,000 miles club and my luggage into the 150,000 miles club."

4
"One advantage of a small car is that you can squeeze twice as many into a traffic jam."

1

Enjoy
Coca-Cola
Trade-mark ®
NO
PARKING
PARTIAL
PICK UP

1

What do you do? Come back tomorrow for the rest of your groceries? "Husbands, don't get so busy earning your salt that you forget your sugar."

2

CHRISTIAN MINISTRY
Parking ONLY
POLICE ENFORCED!

3

NO PARKING TODAY
OR ANY OTHER DAY
IF THAT BIG GREEN
TOW TRUCK HAS NOT
BEEN HERE YET- WORRY
IT WILL BE HERE SOON

2
Does this mean that Christian ministry is police-enforced? (The sign was changed shortly after I took this picture.)

3
It isn't easy to get a parking ticket. First you have to find a parking place.

1

NO PARKING ANY TIME
TOW AWAY ZONE
DON'T EVEN THINK OF PARKING HERE
STOP

1
This was close to President Carter's campaign headquarters in Plains, Georgia. "Buy your wife her favorite flower—Pillsbury."

2

SLOW
Sleeping Policeman

3

SPEED
LIMIT
25
SPEED
LIMIT
45

2
The traffic bump in Jamaica is called a "sleeping policeman."

3
Which? Your choice? "Have you ever been stopped by a state trooper who just wanted to tell you that you are doing an excellent job of not exceeding the speed limit?"

1

65
45
55

2

OPEN
EIGHT DAYS
A WEEK

3

SLOW
14½ MILES
PER HOUR

1
Left eye 65, right eye 55. When speed limit was changed.

2
Service station in Whitehorse, Yukon.

3
It pays to be exact—not 14 or 15. In Guelph, Ontario.

4

CARS PAINTED
29 95
ONE SIDE

5

OPEN 23½ HOURS
EVERYBODY NEEDS
ALITTLE REST

4
"One man had his car painted red on one side and blue on the other. In case of an accident, it would confuse the witness."

5
Open from Sunday through Monday, with a daily one-half hour hiatus. Service station in Mississippi.

1

WE FIX
A CAR
SO IT
BRAKES

1

Smiles are included at this garage. "I am for Santa Claus. Any guy who drops into your house only once a year and doesn't eat or stay over could be my friend for life."

2

FREE ASPIRIN
ASK US ANYTHING

3

KENNETH L. LEHMAN
FREE ASPIRIN &
TENDER SYMPATHY

4

TEXAS
MAR
86
TRAVEL TRAILER
R MOTEL

2
Service station in Las Vegas, Nevada. "The gambler drove his $20,000 Cadillac to Las Vegas and came back in a $100,000 Greyhound."

3
As you leave Las Vegas. "The only way to take a small fortune out of Las Vegas is to take a large fortune in."

4
This license plate was on a motorcycle trailer. "The person with the weakest kidneys is always given a window seat."

1

APR
89
DOIOU 2
INDIANA

2

81 · INDIANA ·
APR
NOP CME

3

APR
WANDER
86
I SUE 4U

1
My license plate.

2
This license plate belongs to Dr. Marx, an outstanding urologist in Lafayette, Indiana.

3
"People begin to find someone to blame and that makes lawyers real happy." "I slept like a lawyer last night. First I would lie on one side, then I would lie on the other side." "There are so many malpractice suits against physicians that if you want an opinion you have to see his lawyers."

4

WE
REBUILD
HEADS
HERE

4
It didn't say what kind of heads, but it was in front of a garage in Georgia. "My mechanic worked on my car and sent a bill for $750.00. He called it open-hood surgery."

Food and Taverns

1

DIESEL
ICE CREAM CONES

2

LEAD·FREE
EXIT
HOT
COFFEE
SANDWICHES·MILK
CIG NO LIMIT ROAD SERVIC
ICE
OVERNIGHT

3

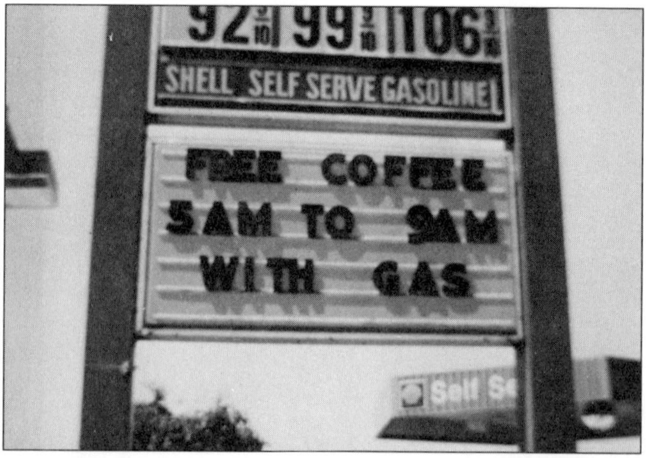
SHELL SELF SERVE GASOLINE
FREE COFFEE
5AM TO 9AM
WITH GAS

1
In front of a combination service station and store in Florida. "Ever taste diesel ice cream?"

2
Could this mean unleaded coffee? No, the word "gas" is in very small letters in North Carolina.

3
You get gas with free coffee in West Palm Beach, Florida.

4

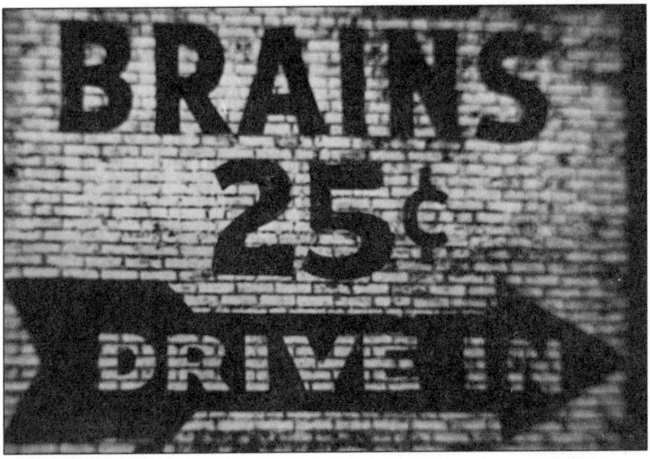
BRAINS
25¢
DRIVE IN

5

SHAISTA
MOTEL $13.95
TRUCK STOP
SHOWER 99¢
80.9 90.9
HAMBURGER

4
"I have been on a diet for four months, and the only thing that gets thin is my hair." "Square meals often make round people."

5
The price of unleaded was $1.169 in Houston, so when I saw this sign in Louisiana, I turned around and filled up. Then when I learned how much I owed and explained the price was only 90.9, the attendant told me the 90.9 referred to a hamburger.

1

PAGODA
ESTAURANT
AIR-CONDITIONED
BELLY DANCERS
ABC ON & OFF NO COVER

2

NO Crabs
after
9:30

3

Grand Cafe
We even eat
here ourselves.

1
What? No cover on the belly dancers? "Do you remember when the only food additives were catsup and mustard?"

2
From a seafood restaurant in Oxford, Maryland. "In order to stay on a diet, a person must follow the path of feast resistance."

3
This was probably the first humorous sign that I saw in Homewood, Illinois, in 1933, my first year out of college. "If God had intended for me to be thin, he never would have given me a skin that stretches."

4

FOLKS
Y'ALL
BE SHORE
T'STOP

5

SO
YA KIN
HELP PAY
FER THE
DERN SIGNS

6

NO TOPLESS
MALE PATRONS

4
On the road to Clewiston, Florida. The barbecue ribs were really tasty.

5
"I eat a well-balanced diet. I just eat it too often."

6
What about the female patrons—in Monticello, Indiana?

1

HOUSE
ORDERS
DAIRY FOODS
The BREAKFAST HOUSE
CHOW
WORTH CROWING ABOUT!
SOME EVEN GRUMBLE

2

fireside dining
another roadside attraction

1
"I am a little depressed today. I looked at my birth certificate and found that I've gained 178 pounds, 4 ounces."

2
The sign was still up after the place burned down.

3

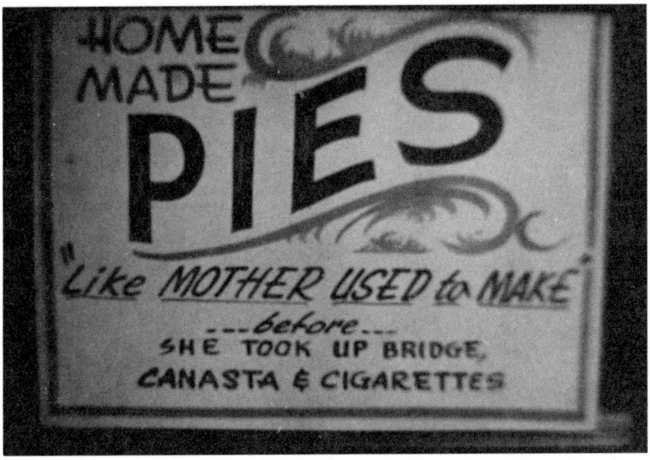
HOME
MADE
PIES
"Like MOTHER USED to MAKE"
---before---
SHE TOOK UP BRIDGE,
CANASTA & CIGARETTES

4

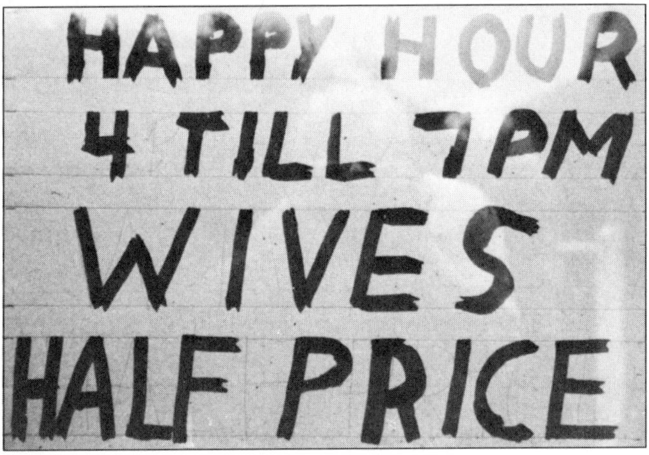
HAPPY HOUR
4 TILL 7PM
WIVES
HALF PRICE

5

SEATING 26,000 (26 AT A TIME
1527

3
"I have always had bad eating habits. Even my food for thought is high in cholesterol."

4
Were wives really half-price during the 4-till-7 happy hour? "Every man needs a wife. He can't blame it all on the government."

5
The restaurant was small, but the owner's humor was big.

1

RESTAURANT
FINE FOOD
BRAS

2

TRAILS END
RESTAURANT
WORLDS SECOND BEST FOODS

1
Shoes a must, bras optional in Skokie, Illinois.

2
Here is one that doesn't claim to be the best. “Confidence is the feeling you sometimes have before you fully understand the situation.”

3

FLORIDA DAIRY STORES
INC.
COLD
BEER

4

DOG
HOUSE
COLD
BEER

5

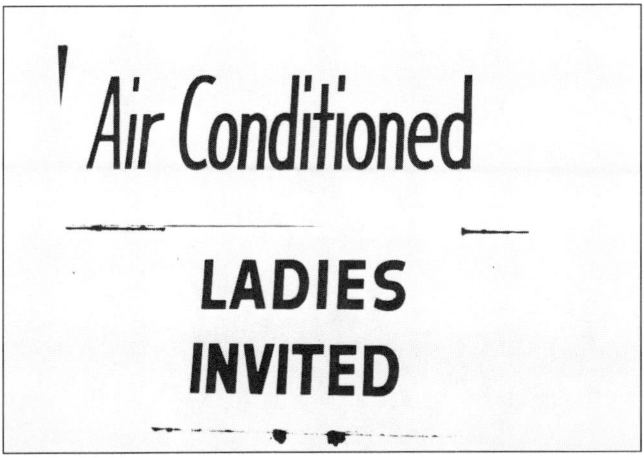
Air Conditioned
LADIES
INVITED

3
What geneticists have accomplished! Now do cows give cold beer?

4
Does your beer taste different lately?

5
Do the ladies really have to be air conditioned in Corydon, Indiana, the state's first capital?

1

Dutch Cupboard
Hind Door
Use Once Der Front

2

ONLY SECOND CLASS
SALOON

1
"Use once der front" in Gettysburg, Pennsylvania. Close to where President Lincoln gave his famous two-hundred-and-sixty-seven-word Gettysburg Address.

2
The honest truth is better than bragging. "It's better to cheat on your diet than cheat on your wife. Never has a chocolate soda hired a lawyer."

3

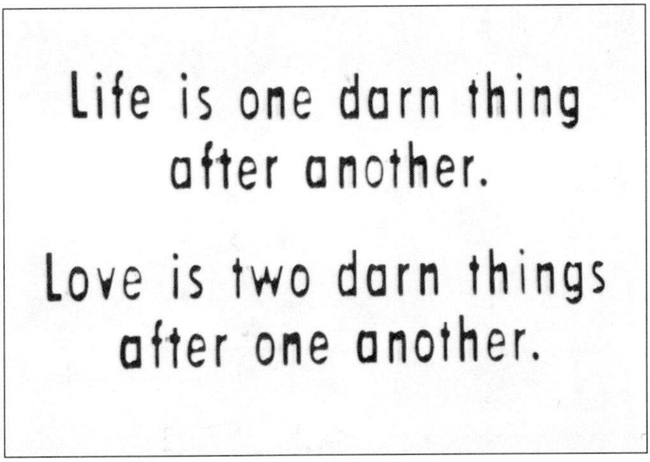
Life is one darn thing
after another.
Love is two darn things
after one another.

4

ALTO
MARRIAGES
& DIVORCES
PARKING

5

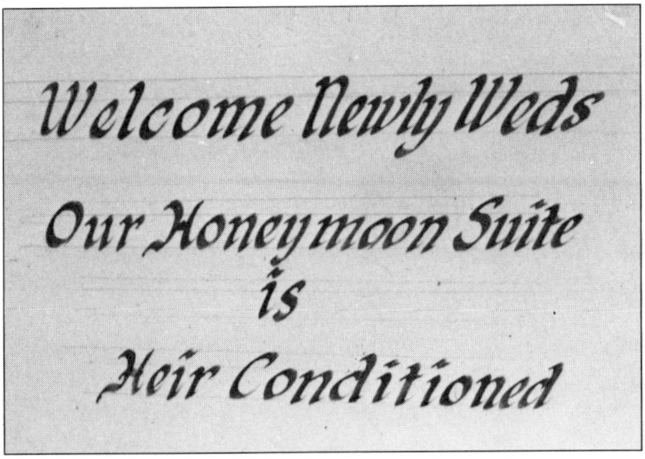
Welcome Newly Weds
Our Honeymoon Suite
is
Heir Conditioned

3
"Fool me once, shame on you. Fool me twice, shame on me." "We do not stop playing when we get old. We get old when we stop playing." "Love quickens all senses, except common sense." "Love is what makes the world go 'round, but it is humor that keeps it from getting dizzier."

4
"Hollywood is where movies have happy marriages and weddings don't, where they take each other for better or for worse—but not for very long." " 'Why do you want a divorce?' 'We have nothing in common. We don't even dislike the same people.' "

5
"Juvenile delinquency is the result of parents trying to raise children without starting at the bottom." "In the good old days before credit cards, men rode chargers. Now they marry them."

WEDDING
CHAPEL
WEDDINGS
PARKING

1
This wedding chapel furnished the license, flowers, minister, witnesses, and photographers. We couldn't use the services since we were already married. Married on MasterCard, Las Vegas.

INDIANA STATE FAIR
INDIANA STATE FAIR
Willing

2
Pillow cases at Indiana state fair. "Horn of plenty" placed third. "Willing" placed first.

FOR TIRED WIVES
FOR BORED HUSBANDS

3
An excellent convenience for tired wives and bored husbands on a Hawaiian vacation. "I bought my wife a new cookbook. It didn't do any good. Her cooking is still bad. She serves milk of magnesia as an after-dinner drink."

4

Dr. A.K. CHU
DENTIST

4

Dr. Chu has his dental office on the island of Molokai. This is not one of the four main islands seen by most visitors to Hawaii. "If time heals, it shouldn't be necessary to go beyond the waiting room in the doctor's office." "A specialist is a doctor who trains his patients to become ill during office hours." "Dentists put your money where your mouth is."

1

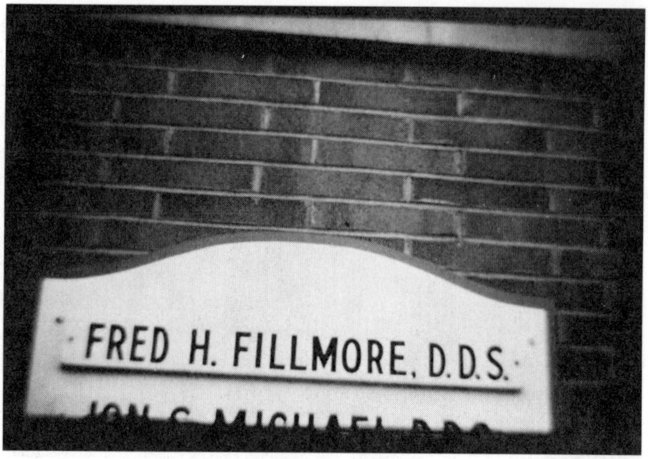
FRED H. FILLMORE, D.D.S.

2

DR.
JOHN A. WINK
OPTOMETRIST

1
Who could be more qualified to fill your teeth than Dr. Fillmore in Lafayette, Indiana? "Another man's toothache doesn't hurt very much."

2
Just wink your eye problems away with Dr. Wink in Davenport, Iowa.

3

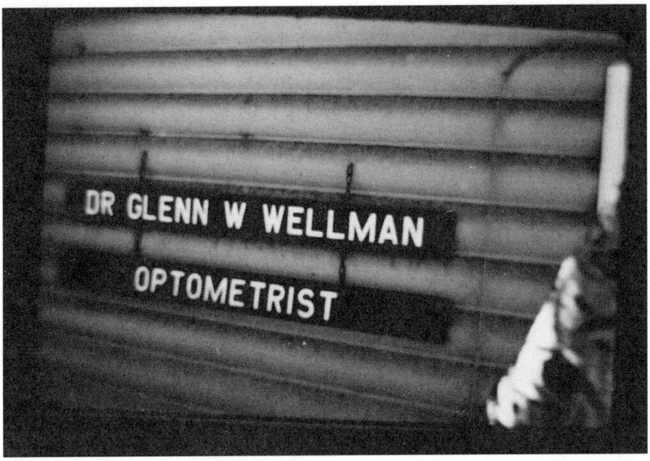
DR GLENN W WELLMAN
OPTOMETRIST

4

ROBERT W. RABBITT, M.D.
OBSTETRICS-GYNECOLOGY

5

BUTCHER'S
MORTUARY

3
"The doctor asked, 'Do you smoke?' 'No.' 'Drink?' 'No.' 'Keep late hours?' 'No.' 'Eat too much?' 'No.' 'How can I cure you if you haven't anything to give up?' "

4
The most logical person to see about a rabbit test certainly must be Dr. Rabbit, an obstetrician and gynecologist in Maryland. "The major side effect of medical treatment today is bankruptcy."

5
"We must not jump to conclusions. Let's not be like the doctor who pronounced the patient dead, only to hear the patient reply, 'I want a second opinion.' "

Funeral Homes

1

Crummy
Funeral Homes

2

JOLLEY
MEMORIAL CHAPEL

3

Deadman
Wash

1
Mr. Crummy is now deceased, but the name will long be remembered. "If I had my life to live over, I would start it much earlier and end it much later."

2
The Jolley funeral home is better than a Sadd funeral home. "Health is wealth and it's tax-free."

3
Does this mean what it says? "Inflation wouldn't be so bad if they only kept the prices down."

4

Barry M. Deap
Funeral Home

5

DIGGS
Funeral Home

6

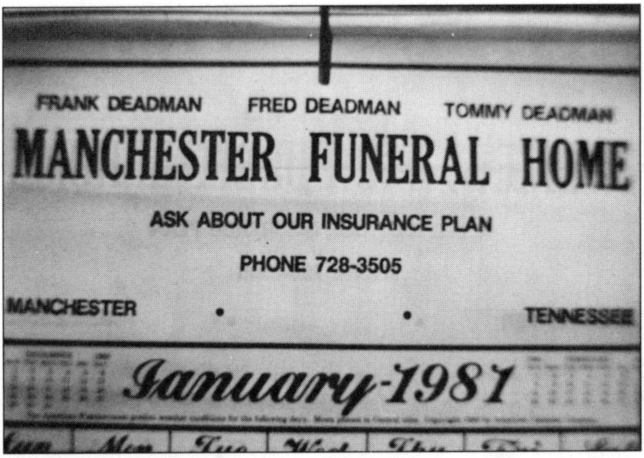
FRANK DEADMAN FRED DEADMAN TOMMY DEADMAN
MANCHESTER FUNERAL HOME
ASK ABOUT OUR INSURANCE PLAN
PHONE 728-3505
MANCHESTER • • TENNESSEE
January-1981

4
The Barry M. Deap Funeral Home sort of speaks for itself.

5
The Diggs Funeral Home was not operated by Digger O'Dell from the old TV show.

6
The Manchester Funeral Home has the same telephone as the Deadman Funeral Home, operated by Frank Deadman, Fred Deadman, and Tommy Deadman. "I am so old that the insurance company sent me one-half of a calendar."

Cemeteries

1

CONCORDIA
CEMETERY
No Articial Flowers
Except Nov.-March
No Planting
Without Permission

2

THOU SHALT NOT DUMP
TRASH IN CEMETERY
VIOLATORS WILL BE
PERSECUTED

3

... NEW ...
PROSPECT
CEMETERY
SIGN & PLANTING
Donated By N.FT. MYERS GARDEN CLUB

1
"The Bible says we bring nothing into this world and take nothing out. So does the IRS."

2
"You are getting old when you look at the menu before you look at the waitress."

3
Everyone seems to be looking for new prospects these days. "There are two political parties—convicted and acquitted."

4

HERE
LIES
LESTER MOORE
FOUR SLUGS
FROM A·44
NO LES
NO MORE

4

One epitaph stated, "I expected this but not so soon." Another said, "This will prove I was here." Another said, "I am a Republican. I never voted Democrat and I never will."

Restrooms and Sanitation

1

SOUTHERN
SANITATION SERVICE
FREE
SNOW
REMOVAL
WE
CATER
WEDDINGS
WE SERVICE WHAT WE SMELL

2

SOUTHERN
SANITATION SERVICE
A Waste Management Company
CAUTION
VEHICLE STOPS AND BACKS FREQUENTLY
THIS TRUCK HAS BAD BREATH
974 7500
CAUTION
DO NOT
PUSH

1
Free snow removal in Southern Florida, where it never snows and they service what they smell.

2
This garbage truck really does have bad breath in Pampano Beach, Florida.

3

HAPPINESS IS
PEACE AND QUIET
AND AN EXTRA ROLL
OF TOILET PAPER

4

HAPPINESS
IS
GETTING HERE
ON TIME!

3
"Happiness is not freedom from problems and difficulties, but it is solving problems and overcoming difficulties."

4
It is especially nice if one has a magazine, too!

1

Put your Trash
into 'Orbit'
5 Minutes

2

ORBIT

1
This was seen on our trip to Alaska in 1967 at the time when Orbit was still in the news.

2
Canadians used a little humor to secure cooperation from the tourists. "Politics is a lot like washing windows. The dirt is always on the other side."

3

REST
ROOMS
BEHIND PALM TREES

4

NEED YOUR
BLADDER
FLATTER
RESTROOMS

5

And they said
that Coca Cola was
the pause that
refreshes!

3
One sign in California said, "For restrooms use stairs." A sign near Wisconsin Dells stated, "For restrooms use road."

4
This one was in the Wall Drug store, Wall, South Dakota. It is worth anyone's time to visit this interesting and enjoyable place.

5
I guess this sign would really apply to all restrooms. "Friends may come and friends may go, but enemies accumulate."

1

AIR MAIL
BILLS
HAPPY MAIL
JUNK MAIL

1
"It has been reported that the average person spends eight months of his life opening junk mail." "Now it costs $1.25 to mail a letter, a quarter for a stamp, and a dollar for a phone call to see if the letter got there." Retired flushables now have a new job.

2

REST ROOMS
PLEASE WAIT
FOR OUR HOST
TO SEAT YOU

3

REST ROOMS
PLEASE
SEAT YOURSELF

2 & 3

These two pictures show what you see when you sit at the table closest to the entrance at this gourmet restaurant in Indianapolis. It wasn't intentional, but you can associate the instructions with the restroom sign on the wall. "A gourmet restaurant is where you pay to undereat."

1

REST
ROOMS
PLUS SALES TAX

1
What? Another sales tax? "The long and short of giving a speech is, the shorter the speech, the longer the applause." Lafayette, Indiana.

2

NOTICE
Effective Jan. 1ST, 1982
PRICE INCREASE
TO $12.00 PER TON
FOR GARBAGE
NO
IVING
LE

2
Are you buying or selling garbage? From Pampano Beach, Florida. "Everything balances out in life. In the first six months of 1987, my ship came in. In the last six months, the stock market unloaded it."

Money

1

OPEN
SUNDAY
NOT-FOR-YOUR
CONVIENCE,
JUST CAUSE
WE NEED THE
MONEY

1
"A wonderful thing about money is that it goes with any outfit you wear."
"Spring cleaning is when my wife cleans out the closet, I clean out the garage, and the IRS cleans out my bank account."

2

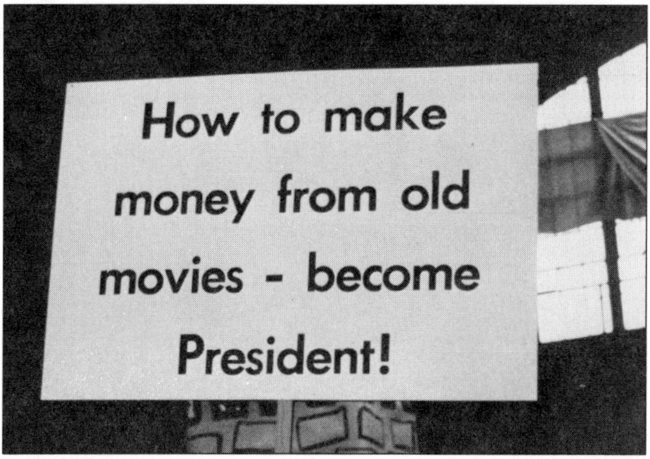
How to make
money from old
movies - become
President!

3

If We Are Closed
Just Shove Your
Money Under
the Door

2
"The President is considering pay raises for some highly skilled workers. This shouldn't cost too much since there aren't many of them." "America is the only country in the world where a person is presumed innocent until the President offers him a job." "If you lie to people to get money—that's fraud. If you lie to people to get votes—that's politics."

3
"I believe in living within my income, even if I have to borrow it to do it." "The income tax form is where taxpayers put two and two together and arrive at minus four."

Antiques

1

THIS IS NOT A
MUSEUM
THIS JUNK IS
FOR SALE

2

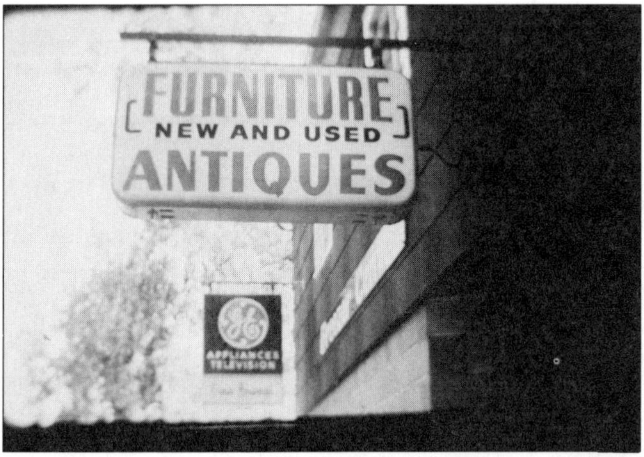
FURNITURE
NEW AND USED
ANTIQUES

3

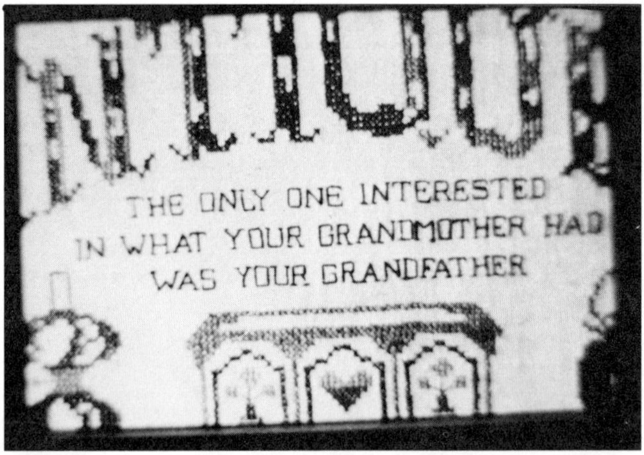
THE ONLY ONE INTERESTED
IN WHAT YOUR GRANDMOTHER HAD
WAS YOUR GRANDFATHER

1
Humor from an antique store owner in Savannah, Georgia. "Happiness is to live as if Moses had made a second trip to Sinai and come back with the ten contentments."

2
One antique store had a sign, "If we don't have it we will make it today and you can get it tomorrow."

3
One antique store had a sign, "$5 extra if we have to listen to what your grandmother had."

4

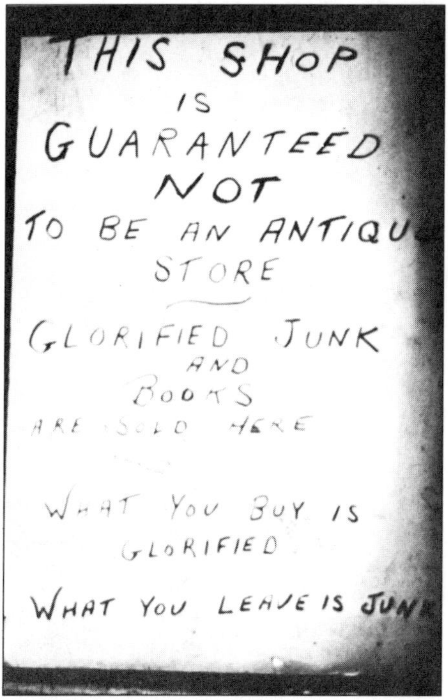
THIS SHOP
IS
GUARANTEED
NOT
TO BE AN ANTIQU
STORE
GLORIFIED JUNK
AND
BOOKS
WHAT YOU BUY IS
GLORIFIED
WHAT YOU LEAVE IS JUN

5

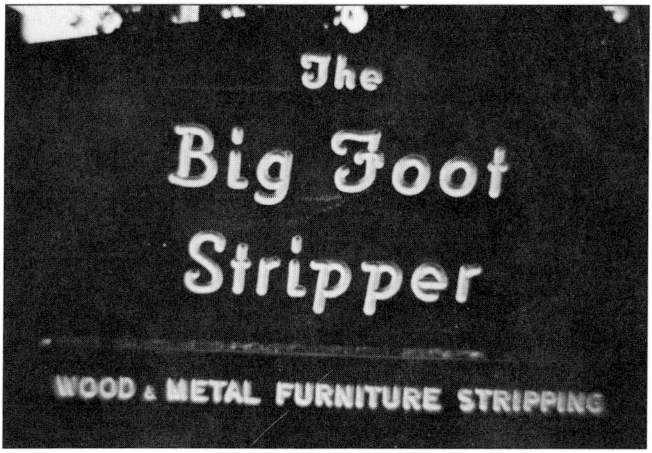
The
Big Foot
Stripper
WOOD & METAL FURNITURE STRIPPING

4
"An antique is something you can't use that can't be fixed at a price you can't afford."

5
Here is just one kind of stripper. "The ultimate in burglar protection would be a sign in every window, 'This house is protected by radon.' "

1

FLEA MARKET
DUMPING
ONLY
DON'T GET
CAUGHT :

1
This gentle hint really carries a neat message. "It sure is tough to pay four dollars for a pound of steak, but it's tougher when you pay only two dollars a pound."

2

HANSEN'S
BARBER SHOP
WE CLIP EVERYBODY

3

DRIVE CAREFULLY
WE CAN WAIT
STILLWELL
MONUMENTAL SALES

4

TO THE BEST

2
"When he said his right ear was warmer than his left, I knew his toupee was on crooked." "The best remedy for gray hair is total baldness."

3
A clever way of suggesting that one drives carefully. "Humor is a way of saying I am sharing something with you that we can both enjoy."

4
Is this the best building? Looks can be deceiving. Actually it was originally an ad for tobacco. "Thank heaven for bad luck. Without it, I wouldn't have any luck at all."

Misinterpretables

1

HUSBAND
EXTERMINATORS
& PEST CONTROL
CERTIFIED PEST CONTROL
OPERATOR
WEEKLY & MONTHLY CONTRACTS

2

BUST
STOP

1
The pest control operator's name is Husband. "I always give my wife her Christmas presents on December 15th. That way she can exchange them in time for Christmas."

2
This bus stop in Warm Springs, Georgia, was seen on the Real People show. "The cheapest place to have Christmas dinner is at Grandma's house—unless you are Grandpa."

3

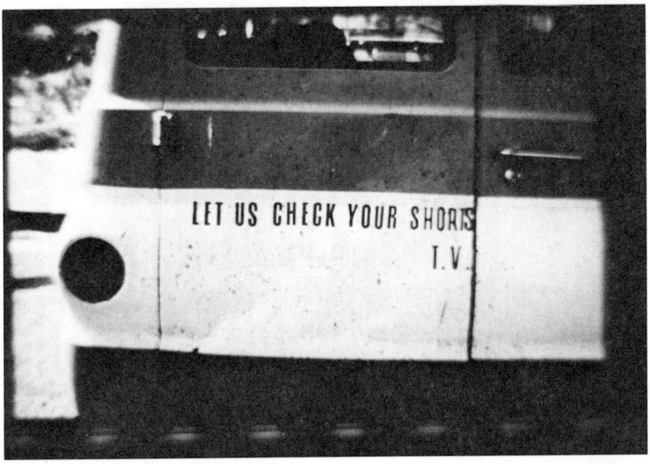
LET US CHECK YOUR SHORTS
T.V.

4

NOTICE
COFFEE IS 10 CENTS
A CUP
15¢ FOR BARBERS ON SATURDAYS
OR DAYS BEFORE HOLIDAYS

3
On the rear door of a TV repair van in Grand Coulee, Washington.

4
This restaurant in Hampshire, Illinois, used a little humor in one of its signs. "My wife and I always have an equitable division of Thanksgiving. She shops, cooks, sets the table, serves the food, cleans up—and I tell her who is winning the game."

1

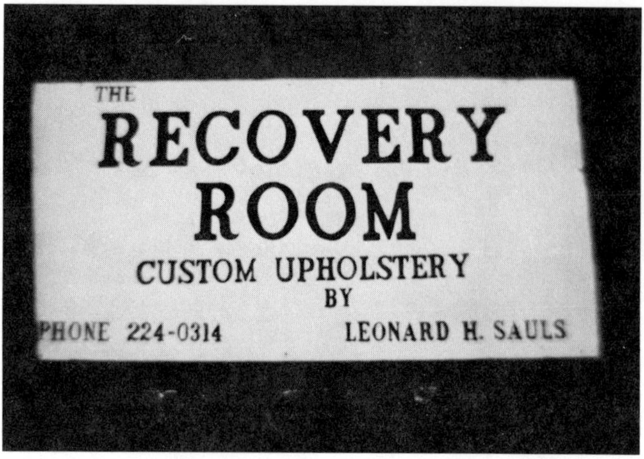
THE
RECOVERY
ROOM
CUSTOM UPHOLSTERY
BY
PHONE 224-0314
LEONARD H. SAULS

2

FLATS FIXED FREE FOR LADIES

3

SOUTH OF THE BORDER
SIGN PLANNED IN WASHINGTON
(Pedro feex later. okay?)

1
Hospitals aren't the only place you will find a recovery room. "More and more hospitals are losing money. Even the blood banks are in the red."

2
Flats fixed free for ladies. Seen near American Falls, Idaho.

3
"The campaign promises of today are the taxes of tomorrow." "Life just isn't fair. Earnings are minus taxes and bills are plus tax." "Politicians don't have to fool all the people—just the 30% that take time to vote."

4

Aladdin
ELECTRIC
Let us remove your shorts
197 656B
GO ILLINI!

5

GRAND OPENING
COME IN
AND HELP PAY FOR
RENT ON THIS SIGN

4
The Aladdin Electric in Champaign, Illinois, offers to remove your shorts.

5
Here is an honest dealer who explains everything. "Never marry for money. It's cheaper to borrow."

1

IMC
NOW HIRING
NOT-HIRING

1
Which part of the sign should you believe? As seen near Indianapolis, Indiana. "Gossip is what you pass on quickly before you find out it's not so."

2

BIG
BUG
FEED

2
Does this really mean feed for big bugs? No, Big Bug is in Arizona, and there is a nearby creek identified as Big Bug Creek.

1

CANTWELL
SLEEP STORES
BEDDING & BRASS

1
You can sleep well when you buy from Cantwell Sleep. "Let me make one thing clear. I do not oversleep. I under-awake."

2

HIS
HERS

2
Women's Lib for the lady horses in this horse pasture near Lafayette, Indiana.

3

HEADQUARTERS
FOR
HINDQUARTERS

3
Headquarters for hindquarters in Oregon. "A taxpayer is one who doesn't have to take a civil service exam to work for the government."

4

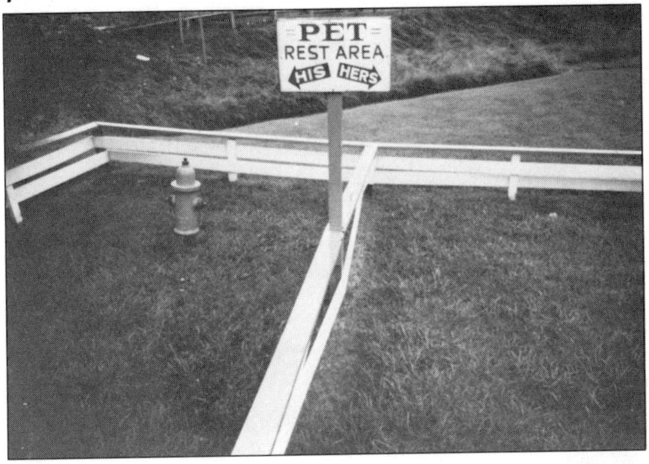
PET
REST AREA
HIS
HERS

5

1/4
HORSE
SALE

4
This service station east of Columbus, Ohio, offers a complete service. "Candidates are people who tell you everything they know and then keep on talking."

5
It's one-fourth horse for sale on one side, but a quarter horse on the other side. "If you can't say something nice about a person, don't waste it. Talk about the candidates."

1

DROP
YOUR
PANTS
HERE!

1
This dry cleaner in Indianapolis really draws your attention. "The modern bathtub was invented in 1856. The telephone was invented in 1870. That means that for fourteen years you could soak peacefully without being called to the telephone."

2

CHUCK HALL'S
BOARDING STABLES
NEW & USED HORSES FOR SALE
964-8253

3

ENERGY EFFICIENT
VEHICLE.
RUNS ON OATS AND GRASS.
CAUTION DO NOT
STEP ON EXHAUST
Yellow Rose
Carriages

4

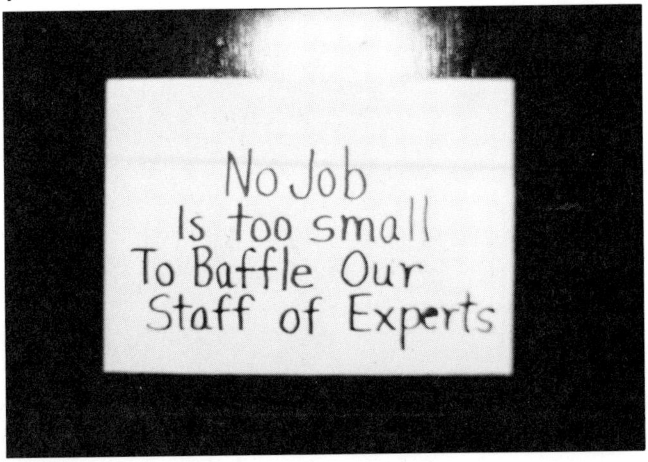
No Job
Is too small
To Baffle Our
Staff of Experts

2
Take your choice, new or used horses, near Mesa, Arizona. "I want my children to have all the things I couldn't afford. Then I want to move in with them."

3
The EPA does not monitor all exhausts. "An authority is a person who can tell you more about something than you really want to know."

4
Humor in the workplace. "Susan B. Anthony was arrested in 1872 in New York for attempting to vote."

1

I'M SO FULL OF
WORRIES
THAT IF SOMETHING
HAPPENS TODAY I
WON'T HAVE TIME
TO WORRY ABOUT IT
UNTIL NEXT MONTH

1
"The nice thing about trivia is that it keeps us from worrying about important problems."
"The optimist is often as wrong as the pessimist—but he is far happier."

2

200 YEARS AGO TODAY
NOTHING HAPPENED HERE
IT WILL NOW

3

PERSONNEL
ONLY

2
Humor expressed in Stockwell, Texas. "By the time most people can afford children they are grandparents."

3
On mayor's former office in Orlando, Florida. "The difference between a job and a career is about 20 hours a week."

1

WELCOME
THIS COLONIAL HOUSE WAS BUILT
IN THE GAY 90s IT HAS NO PARTICULAR
HISTORY EXCEPT "RIP VAN WINKLE"
SLEPT HERE.
905
RUE ROYAL

2

KINDLY PARK
YORE CIGAR
OUTSIDE

1
And a little humor in New Orleans. "If you wonder why Aaron made a golden calf, it was because he didn't have enough gold for a cow."

2
Cigars were not welcome in this restaurant in Central City, Colorado. "I won't say it was a cheap restaurant, but they only had two beans in their three-bean salad."

3

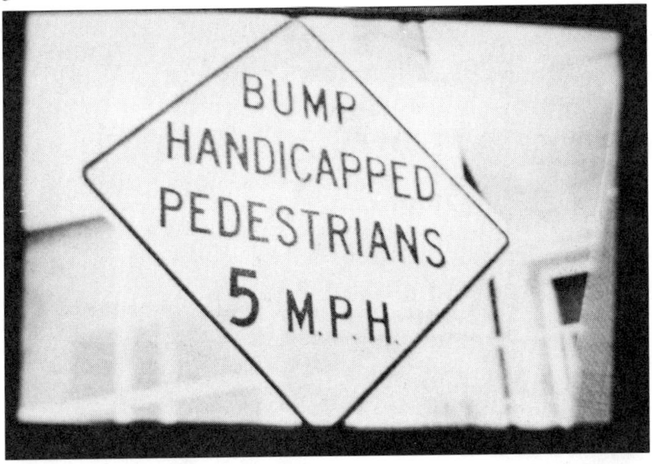
BUMP
HANDICAPPED
PEDESTRIANS
5 M.P.H.

4

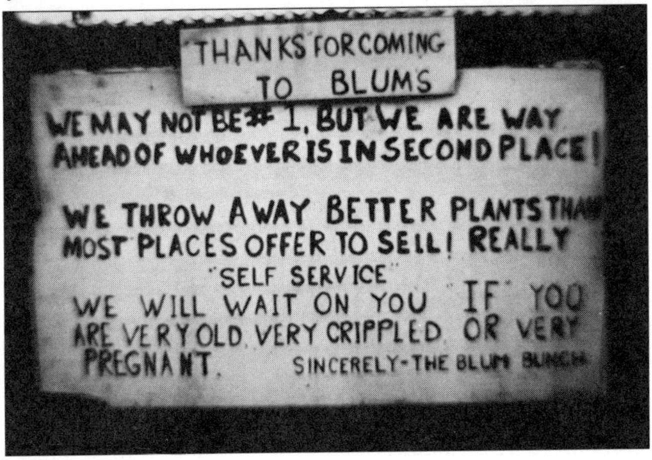
THANKS FOR COMING
TO BLUMS
WE MAY NOT BE # 1, BUT WE ARE WAY
AHEAD OF WHOEVER IS IN SECOND PLACE!
WE THROW AWAY BETTER PLANTS THAN
MOST PLACES OFFER TO SELL! REALLY
"SELF SERVICE"
WE WILL WAIT ON YOU IF YOU
ARE VERY OLD. VERY CRIPPLED. OR VERY
PREGNANT.
SINCERELY-THE BLUM BUNCH

3
Is it all right to bump the non-handicapped pedestrians? "How come vices are more habit-forming than virtues?"

4
"Happiness would be a government that lived within its income and without mine."

1

BONANZA BEN
LARGEST REAL IMITATION
GOLD NUGGET EVER FOUND

1
This gold-colored rock brings smiles to visitors in Ketchikan, Alaska. "Self-confidence is when you hope you are right 100% of the time, sometimes more."

2

Dough Belly's
CLIP JOINT
REAL ESTATE

3

NON CHEMICAL
WEED
CONTROL

2
Honest advertising in New Mexico. "Income is something you cannot live without or within."

3
Here is the answer for those who object to chemical weed control. "Some goats don't seem to understand the definition of a weed." "Two things are universal—hydrogen and stupidity."

1

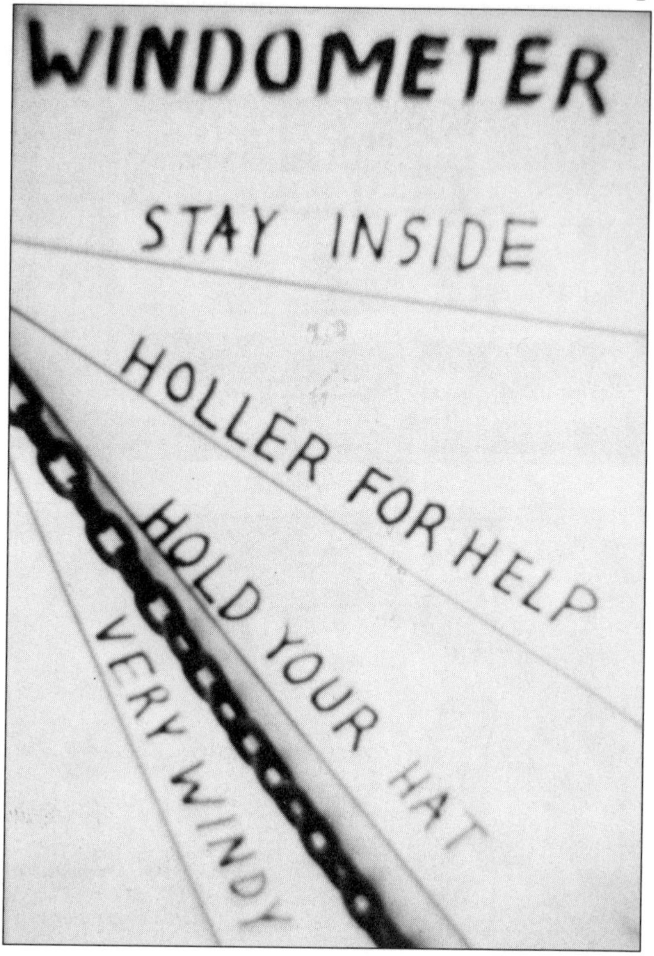
WINDOMETER
STAY INSIDE
HOLLER FOR HELP
HOLD YOUR HAT
VERY WINDY

1
Sometimes the wind blows pretty hard. Now you can check it by this log chain. "Homeowners spend an enormous amount of time, money, and effort to have a luxurious lawn and then complain about mowing the grass."

2

PLEASE SOUND HORN
TO WAKE ATTENDANT

3

KEEP OFF
THE GRASS

2
Hawaiians express a little humor in this sign. "A committee is a group of people who individually can do nothing, but as a group decide nothing can be done."

3
It was all rocks, no grass, at Great Bear Lake, north of the Arctic Circle where I went fishing. The management liked to see smiles on the faces of their guests. Northwest Territory.

1

SINNER'S
PHARMACY

2

SLOW DOWN
SMILE
YOU ARE ON
RADAR

1
A special pharmacy for those who sin a little? No, the owner's name is Sinner, in Mattoon, Illinois. "Retirement is when you wonder why they are called easy chairs when they are so hard to get out of."

2
The town of Greenfield, Indiana, has a subtle way of telling you to obey the speed limit. "Retirement is that period in life when you finally get it all together and are giving it to the doctors."

3

ALL OF OUR
CUSTOMERS MAKE
US HAPPY.
SOME WHEN THEY
ARRIVE AND
SOME WHEN THEY
LEAVE!

3
This sign was in an antique store in Intercourse, Pennsylvania. "I worked hard to put two children through college—my doctor's."

1

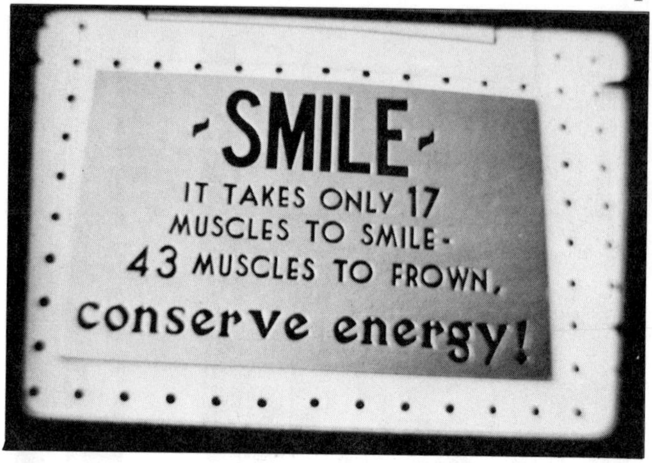
SMILE
IT TAKES ONLY 17
MUSCLES TO SMILE-
43 MUSCLES TO FROWN,
conserve energy!

2

I SURVIVED
THE STOCK MARKET
CRASH OF 1987.
I USED TO DRIVE
A CADILLAC.

1
"A smile is a gentle curve that sets a lot of things straight." "Retirement is when every day is Saturday."

2
This fellow put a little humor on his bicycle—after the 1987 stock market crash. "The real secret of waiting is to find something else to do in the meantime."

3

Sorry... we're
Closed
OPEN

3

Is the store closed, or is it open? You just can't believe everything you see or hear. "Christmas is when you get the impression that God created the world in six days—and on the seventh day created batteries to make it all work."

About the author

Walter Weber is an entomologist and teacher by training, a photographer by hobby, a speaker and writer by choice. He is an alumnus of the University of Illinois with a Masters Degree from Purdue University. He has carried a camera to all fifty states and several foreign countries.

Walter is a registered professional entomologist, a member of the Indiana Academy of Science, the National Speakers Association, and the Lutheran Church.

Walter is the author of *The Unflushables: Outhouses—History and Humor*. It represents a slice of American history that is rapidly disappearing. The more than one hundred pictures include two-, three-, and five-story outhouses along with those of presidents and many preserved by historical and preservation societies. He is the co-author of *Funnybones: Health and Humor Experts*.

Walter invites you to his one-hundredth birthday, January 6, 2011. He lives at 36 West Roberts Road, Indianapolis, IN; phone (317) 786-7251.

Back Home Again
89
DO I OU 2
INDIANA